Vice President, Licensing & Publishing Amanda Joiner
Editorial Manager Carrie Bolin

Editor Jordie R. Orlando
Writer Korynn Wible-Freels
Designer Luis Fuentes
Reprographics Bob Prohaska

Published by Ripley Publishing 2020

10 9 8 7 6 5 4 3 2 1

Copyright © 2020 Ripley Publishing

ISBN: 978-1-60991-447-9

For more information regarding permission, contact:
VP Licensing & Publishing
Ripley Entertainment Inc.
7576 Kingspointe Parkway, Suite 188
Orlando, Florida 32819

Email: publishing@ripleys.com
www.ripleys.com/books
Manufactured in China in January 2020.

First Printing

Library of Congress Control Number: 2019942267

PUBLISHER'S NOTE
While every effort has been made to verify the accuracy of the entries in this book, the Publisher cannot be held responsible for any errors contained in the work. They would be glad to receive any information from readers.

PHOTO CREDITS

4-5 © Ewelina Wachala/Shutterstock.com; **6-7** © Gaid Kornsilapa/Shutterstock.com; **8-9** (t) © Martyn Skorkin/Shutterstock.com; **8-9** (b) © reddees/Shutterstock.com; **10-11** © JHVEPhoto/Shutterstock.com; **12** © Allard One/Shutterstock.com; **13** © jean morrison/Shutterstock.com; **14** © joyfull/Shutterstock.com; **15** © bkueskiesescapes/Shutterstock.com; **16-17** © Kenneth Sponsler/Shutterstock.com; **18** © Larry Porges/Shutterstock.com; **19** MERCURY PRESS via Caters; **20** © Bilal Kocabas/Shutterstock.com; **21** © Bilal Kocabas/Shutterstock.com; **24-25** © Chris Howey/Shutterstock.com; **25** © Matyas Rehak/Shutterstock.com; **26-27** © serkan senturk/Shutterstock.com; **28** © O.C Ritz/Shutterstock.com; **29** © Abd. Halim Hadi/Shutterstock.com; **Master Graphics** © SNEHIT/Shutterstock.com

Key: t = top, b = bottom, c = center, l = left, r = right, sp = single page, bkg = background

All other photos are from Ripley Entertainment Inc.

Every attempt has been made to acknowledge correctly and contact copyright holders, and we apologize in advance for any unintentional errors or omissions, which will be corrected in future editions.

LEXILE®, LEXILE FRAMEWORK®, LEXILE ANALYZER®, the LEXILE® logo and POWERV® are trademarks of MetaMetrics, Inc., and are registered in the United States and abroad. The trademarks and names of other companies and products mentioned herein are the property of their respective owners. Copyright © 2019 MetaMetrics, Inc. All rights reserved.

Ripley Readers

Bizarre Buildings

All true and unbelievable!

RIPLEY
PUBLISHING

a Jim Pattison Company

Who says that buildings
have to look the same?

Let's go around the world
to find cool buildings!

Some buildings are made
to look like animals.
The "Toad King Museum"
is the king of toads, indeed!

The perfect place to
talk about seafood is
inside this giant fish!

Woof woof! Dog lovers can stay the night in this fun building.

Other buildings are made to look like food. This giant apple can hold *half a million* real apples!

People go nuts for donuts at this donut shop! You can drive through the middle to pick up your food.

It was an old tradition to put fruit on the front gate. This pineapple house takes that to the next level!

Are you scared of heights?
This building is very tall.

It has a giant pool
on the 57th floor!

Some buildings look like things you can find in your home.

Do you have a picnic basket?
How about one with handles
that weigh 150 tons?

This boot-shaped house
is a fairy tale come to life.

You are not seeing things.
This house was built to look
upside down!

Even the inside is topsy-turvy!

Buildings can be made from strange things.

That is not firewood. It is a house inside a redwood tree!

Believe it or not... Redwood trees can grow as tall as a building and live for 2,000 years!

Will you pass the salt?
Wait, this hotel is made of
it! Even the walls, floors,
and beds are made with salt.

Why stay at a normal hotel when you can stay at one of these?

Take extra blankets when you visit this ice hotel. It gets remade every winter.

Can you see the treehouse?
The mirrors make it blend in
with the forest!

A hotel in the middle of the ocean? That's right! This oil rig is now a hotel for scuba divers.

Believe it or not... Ripley's has a lot of neat buildings, too!

This one looks like wild woods with fun animals!

A big robot sits on top of this one!

There are so many bizarre buildings!

Ready for More?

Ripley Readers feature unbelievable but true facts and stories!

LEVEL ONE — Sounding it out

LEVEL TWO — Reading with help

LEVEL THREE — Independent reading

LEVEL FOUR — Chapters

   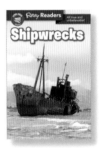

**For more information about
Ripley's Believe It or Not!, go to www.ripleys.com**